Written by Carol Murray
Illustrated by Dave Garbot

Children's Press®
A Division of Scholastic Inc.
New York • Toronto • London • Auckland • Sydney
Mexico City • New Delhi • Hong Kong
Danbury, Connecticut

To Megan, Alex, and Ashley, my wonderful grandchildren
—C.M.

To Brandon, my best friend and inspiration
—D.G.

3 3113 02326 6994   Reading Consultants

Linda Cornwell
Literacy Specialist

Katharine A. Kane
Education Consultant
(Retired, San Diego County Office of Education and San Diego State University)

Library of Congress Cataloging-in-Publication Data

Murray, Carol.
 Hurry up! / written by Carol Murray ; illustrated by Dave Garbot.
  p. cm. — (Rookie reader)
Summary: A child's teeth must be brushed, hair combed, and bed made before
he goes to the circus.
 ISBN 0-516-22585-5 (lib. bdg.)   0-516-27831-2 (pbk.)
 [1. Behavior—Fiction. 2. Circus—Fiction. 3. Stories in rhyme.] I.Garbot, Dave, ill.
II. Title. III. Series.
 PZ8.3.M936 Hu 2003
 [E]— dc21

                    2002008798

"Brush those teeth," Aunt Ella said.

"Comb that hair upon your head."

"Wash your hands and make your bed.
And hurry up!" Aunt Ella said.

"I have a big surprise for you.
So, hurry, hurry, hurry, do!"

So, I brush my teeth.

I comb my hair.

I wipe some toothpaste off the chair.

I wash my hands.

I make my bed,
just like my Auntie Ella said.

I hurry up,
pick up my toys,
and make an awful lot of noise.

I look about my tidy room.

We're out of here!
Zoom! Zoom! Zoom!

And soon we spy some circus tents.
The clowns, the bears, the elephants!

TICKETS

"Thanks, Aunt El, for taking me.
This is a super sight to see."

"And thanks," she said, with twinkly eye,
"for being such a speedy guy!"

31

Word List (79 words)

a	do	like	so	tidy
about	El	look	some	to
an	elephants	lot	soon	toothpaste
and	Ella	make	speedy	toys
Aunt	eye	me	spy	twinkly
Auntie	for	my	such	up
awful	guy	noise	super	upon
bears	hair	of	surprise	wash
bed	hands	off	taking	we
being	have	out	teeth	we're
big	head	pick	tents	wipe
brush	here	room	thanks	with
chair	hurry	said	that	you
circus	I	see	the	your
clowns	is	she	this	zoom
comb	just	sight	those	

About the Author

Carol Murray is a teacher and a published poet. She taught English and Speech at Hutchinson Community College for twenty-five years. She lives in the country in Kansas, with her husband, Max, and two quarter horses named Lucky and Bud. Her favorite animal is the giraffe. She especially likes kids and poetry and black and white cats.

About the Illustrator

Dave Garbot lives and works in Portland, Oregon. He has been drawing for as long as he can remember and always kind of knew he would be an artist. He feels the best part of his job is creating images that will make his audience smile and feel happy.